INSIDE MLS

COLORADO
RAPIDS

BY ANTHONY K. HEWSON

SportsZone
An Imprint of Abdo Publishing
abdobooks.com

abdobooks.com

Published by Abdo Publishing, a division of ABDO, PO Box 398166, Minneapolis, Minnesota 55439. Copyright © 2022 by Abdo Consulting Group, Inc. International copyrights reserved in all countries. No part of this book may be reproduced in any form without written permission from the publisher. SportsZone™ is a trademark and logo of Abdo Publishing.

Printed in the United States of America, North Mankato, Minnesota
052021
092021

Cover Photo: David Zalubowski/AP Images
Interior Photos: Jack Dempsey/AP Images, 4–5, 7, 11, 15, 30; Nathan Denette/The Canadian Press/AP Images, 8; Denver Post/Getty Images, 13; David Zalubowski/AP Images, 17, 21, 40, 43; Winslow Townson/AP Images, 18; Ben Nelms/The Canadian Press/AP Images, 23; Chris Putnam/AP Images, 25; Adrian Wyld/The Canadian Press/AP Images, 27; Tyler Mallory/AP Images, 29; Hyoung Chang/MediaNews Group/The Denver Post/Getty Images, 33; Jed Jacobsohn/Allsport/Getty Images, 35; Stephen Dunn/Getty Images Sport/Getty Images, 37; Andy Lyons/Getty Images Sport/Getty Images, 39

Editor: Patrick Donnelly
Series Designer: Dan Peluso

Library of Congress Control Number: 2020948260

Publisher's Cataloging-in-Publication Data

Names: Hewson, Anthony K., author.
Title: Colorado Rapids / by Anthony K. Hewson
Description: Minneapolis, Minnesota : Abdo Publishing, 2022 | Series: Inside MLS | Includes online resources and index.
Identifiers: ISBN 9781532194719 (lib. bdg.) | ISBN 9781098214371 (ebook)
Subjects: LCSH: Colorado Rapids (Soccer team)--Juvenile literature. | Soccer teams--Juvenile literature. | Professional sports franchises--Juvenile literature. | Sports Teams--Juvenile literature.
Classification: DDC 796.334--dc23

TABLE OF CONTENTS

CHAPTER 1

ATOP THE
MOUNTAIN

Simply making the playoffs was a big achievement for the 2010 Colorado Rapids. The club had not qualified for the Major League Soccer (MLS) postseason since 2006. Making it to the playoffs meant progress. But once there, few people expected Colorado to do much winning.

The 2010 Rapids finished with the seventh-best record in the league. But due to the playoff format, they got a bit of a break. Rather than playing a top team from the stronger Western Conference, they got to play the second-best team from the Eastern Conference. That was the Columbus Crew. The Crew had won only two more games than Colorado had.

The Rapids lacked star power, but they were a balanced team. They had a creative playmaker in defensive midfielder

Rapids goalkeeper Matt Pickens, left, leaps over a crowd to make a save against the Columbus Crew in the 2010 MLS playoffs.

Pablo Mastroeni. They had a shutdown defender in Marvell Wynne. In goal, Matt Pickens was as strong as anyone in the league. And when it came to scoring, Conor Casey had been their man for years.

SURVIVING AND THRIVING

The Columbus series was anything but easy. After a tough 1–0 win in the first game, Colorado had to survive a penalty shootout in Game 2 to advance. It was only after the Crew's Brian Carroll missed his final attempt that the Rapids ensured their survival.

In the conference finals, the Rapids faced the San Jose Earthquakes in a one-game knockout match. San Jose had the same number of standings points as the Rapids. It wasn't easy, but Colorado scored another 1–0 win to make it back to the MLS Cup for the first time since 1997.

Colorado played FC Dallas in the final. Dallas had won the same number of games as the Rapids did in the regular season, so the final was tough to predict. Both clubs were eager to prove they deserved to be champions. The Rapids knew they weren't the most talented team in MLS. But they believed in themselves.

Conor Casey, *left*, and Omar Cummings celebrate after the Rapids scored the only goal in their victory over San Jose.

Rapids players congratulate Macoumba Kandji after he helped put Colorado on top in stoppage time.

The match took place on November 21 in Toronto. It was one of the coldest finals in history. The Rapids looked like they were the team that needed to heat up. They allowed several Dallas scoring chances in the opening minutes.

Colorado soon shifted to a more defensive style. But it wasn't enough to prevent Dallas from taking the lead in the 35th minute. MLS Most Valuable Player (MVP) David Ferreira buried goal off a crossing pass. Colorado would have some work to do in the second half.

CASEY AT THE GOAL

Casey became the club's all-time leading scorer that season. And in the club's biggest-ever match, he came up big again. In the 57th minute, Casey received a pass in the penalty box. He and Dallas goalkeeper Kevin Hartman went for it at the same time. Both players went to the ground. Still on his back, Casey kicked the ball into the net. The Rapids had tied it 1–1.

Neither team could score a winning goal in regulation, so extra time was needed. The match's most critical and strangest moment came in the second extra 15-minute period.

Colorado forward Macoumba Kandji dribbled the ball into the Dallas box. As a Dallas player arrived to challenge him,

WINNING WHEN IT COUNTS

Kandji punched at the ball with his left foot. The ball bounced off Dallas defender George John and into the goal.

The Rapids players celebrated their good fortune and their 2–1 lead. But they saw Kandji was hurt. It turned out to be a serious knee injury. Colorado was out of substitutes. Kandji stayed on the field, but he couldn't really play. The Rapids had to ride out the final 13 minutes with only 10 healthy players.

It was an intense finish. Dallas kept up the pressure. Pickens made several big saves. Defenders cleared balls from the goal line. Players were diving to the ground and giving their all.

Finally, they heard the sweet sound of the referee's whistle. After 15 years in MLS, the Rapids were finally champions. Kandji was sad that he could not contribute in the match's final moments. But he wouldn't have traded it for anything.

"The [injury] will heal and you will be back playing again, but the championship is going to last forever," Kandji said.

Colorado captain Pablo Mastroeni raises the trophy at a rally to celebrate the Rapids' 2010 MLS Cup victory.

CHAPTER 2

RIDING THE
RAPIDS

The Colorado pro sports landscape changed dramatically over just three years in the 1990s. Not since gold was discovered in the state in the 1850s had there been a bigger surge of a new industry. It started with baseball's Colorado Rockies beginning play in 1993. They then moved into their new ballpark in downtown Denver in 1995, the same year hockey's Quebec Nordiques moved in and became the Colorado Avalanche.

The very same summer, MLS announced that Colorado would have a team in the league's first season in 1996. Denver was clearly a booming sports town, but it didn't have much of a history with pro soccer. It had a pair of pro teams in the North American Soccer League (NASL) in the 1970s.

Jomo Sono of the Caribous of Colorado dribbles through the Los Angeles Aztecs defense in 1978.

But neither the Denver Dynamos nor the memorably named Caribous of Colorado lasted for more than two seasons. The Caribous were best known for the jerseys they wore that had fake leather fringes on the chest.

Nonetheless, there were plenty of soccer fans waiting to embrace their new MLS team. A crowd of 21,711 came out to see the first home game in Rapids history, a 3–1 win over the Dallas Burn. Unfortunately, that proved to be a rare victory that season. Colorado finished in last place and missed the playoffs.

RISE AND FALL

Not wanting to experience such a season again, the Rapids made big changes for 1997. They hired a new general manager and a new coach. They brought in new players. Proven scorers Paul Bravo and Wolde Harris joined the squad. US national team reserve goalkeeper Marcus Hahnemann was a new starter in net. The club not only made the playoffs, it made it all the way to the MLS Cup before falling just short of a title.

The Rapids were an up-and-down team over the next decade. Except for a run to the 1999 US Open Cup final, the team did not play for any trophies. It was frequently a playoff team but never a serious contender.

US men's national team standout Pablo Mastroeni, *left*, joined the Rapids in 2002 and brought stability to the team for 12 years.

It was not that Colorado lacked talent. One of the greatest players ever to suit up for the Rapids roamed midfield during this era. Pablo Mastroeni was a legendary player for both the Rapids and a key contributor to the US national team.

One of Colorado's problems was its stadium. From the outset, the Rapids had shared a stadium with the Denver Broncos. Even moving with the Broncos into a new stadium in 2002 didn't help much. It was brand new, but the stadium was designed for American football. It held more than 70,000 fans. Even with a good Rapids crowd of 20,000, the stadium felt empty to the players.

MLS was changing. Teams were moving into stadiums designed just for soccer. They were smaller and provided fans with an up-close experience.

A NEW ERA

In 2003 businessman Stan Kroenke bought the Rapids. One of his immediate goals was to start building a new soccer-specific stadium. Kroenke was an experienced owner. He and his company owned the Avalanche, basketball's Denver Nuggets, and the arena the teams shared.

Workers prepare for the opening of the Rapids' new stadium in April 2007.

Construction began on the new stadium in 2005. Located in the suburb of Commerce City, Dick's Sporting Goods Park opened for the 2007 season. The club made some other tweaks, such as changing its colors from black and blue to sky blue and burgundy. It also formed a developmental partnership with English Premier League club Arsenal. Kroenke was a part owner of that team, too.

Conor Casey makes a leaping header against the New England Revolution in 2009.

Kroenke's funding and relationships had the club aiming for big things. The Rapids did not make a playoff appearance in 2007, but they did acquire one of the team's greatest players in Conor Casey. They also brought in forward Omar Cummings. Both players would rewrite the Colorado record books.

Casey and Cummings formed one of the best attacking duos in MLS. In 2009 they combined for 24 goals. In 2010 that number surged to 27. No pair of teammates combined for more. That firepower helped boost the Rapids back to the MLS Cup.

Casey was a big part of the team's run to its first championship. He scored two of the Rapids' five playoff goals, including the tying goal in the final. Another big factor was longtime team captain Mastroeni. He scored the match-winner in the conference semifinals that helped get Colorado's playoff run off to a winning start.

REBUILDING

The Rapids returned home with the MLS Cup trophy and were greeted by hundreds of fans. Later that month, 1,000 fans gathered at the state capitol building for Colorado Rapids Day. Hopes were high that more championships were on the way.

However, the Rapids could not sustain the success they had in 2010. By 2012 they were back to missing the playoffs. Casey was released and Cummings was traded after the season. Mastroeni was traded in 2013. Almost all the core players from the MLS Cup team were gone.

Mastroeni soon returned. But it was on the sideline as head coach. He took the reins in 2014. A former US national team player himself, Mastroeni got the help of a couple national teamers after two seasons missing the playoffs.

Colorado traded for US midfielder Jermaine Jones just before the 2016 season. Jones scored 21 minutes into his Rapids debut. Colorado got a bigger boost when goalkeeper Tim Howard joined the club at midseason. Howard and Jones were both huge parts of the US team that advanced to the knockout round at the 2014 World Cup. Howard nearly carried his team into the quarterfinals with a record-setting 15-save performance against Belgium.

Colorado went on a club-record 15-match unbeaten streak. In October the Rapids were vying for the best record in all of MLS. They finished just short but were strong contenders in the playoffs.

The Rapids welcomed US national team hero Tim Howard to the team on June 28, 2016.

Yet the Rapids' run nearly ended quickly. They lost 1–0 in the first match of their series with the LA Galaxy. The Rapids returned home to Colorado needing a win. They won the match 1–0, but that only tied the aggregate score. The match ended up going to a shootout, which Colorado won in one of the most thrilling moments in team history.

THE ROCKY MOUNTAIN CUP

For years, the Rapids were pretty far geographically from their nearest competition. That changed in 2005 when Real Salt Lake joined the league. A rivalry was instantly born. The teams play each year for the Rocky Mountain Cup. The team with the most points in their head-to-head matches each year wins the cup. After Colorado won the first two years, however, the Rapids didn't win for a third time until 2020.

But the Rapids advanced no further. Jones left after the season, but the team still seemed well set up for the future. Instead, Colorado won only nine games in 2017, and Mastroeni was fired.

PLANNING FOR THE FUTURE

Fans began to get frustrated. They were disappointed in the team's ownership. It had failed to build a team that could win consistently. Some fans felt Kroenke did not pay enough attention to the Rapids. Kroenke had become the majority owner of Arsenal and the National Football League's St. Louis Rams since buying the Rapids. Colorado fans felt ignored in comparison to his other teams.

After another losing season in 2018 and a winless start to 2019, the club looked to another team legend to turn things around. Conor Casey was named interim coach. Despite the 0–7–2 start, Casey got the Rapids playing well again, and they

Rookie Andre Shinyashiki finished the 2019 season with seven goals and three assists.

even got back in the playoff race. Big crowds also started to come back to Dick's Sporting Goods Park.

Casey's permanent replacement was Robin Fraser. He took over in August and won five of seven matches. Andre Shinyashiki was named the league's Rookie of the Year. The Rapids did even better in 2020, reaching the playoffs for the first time in four years. After some down years, things were starting to look up once again in Colorado.

CHAPTER 3

RAPIDS
ROYALTY

Marcelo Balboa was there from the very beginning. But just barely. Balboa joined the Rapids three days before the team's first-ever home match. But the defender made his presence felt. He scored two goals that day.

Balboa brought some star power to the new team. With his smart defensive play and signature long, dark hair, he became well known as a member of the US national team. He made his national team debut in 1988 and made more than 125 appearances through 2000. Despite starring for his home country, Balboa wasn't able to pursue a professional career at home because the United States had no major pro league for most of that time. It wasn't until MLS began play

Marcelo Balboa participates in the skills challenge at the 2000 MLS All-Star Game.

in 1996 that he could finally play top-level professional soccer on home soil.

Balboa played 151 games for the Rapids. He helped them make the 1997 MLS Cup final and also scored one of the most iconic goals in league history in 2000. Against the Columbus Crew, Balboa was waiting for a crossing pass in the box. He jumped in the air and performed a bicycle kick, tumbling backward while meeting the ball with his foot. The amazing play was named MLS Goal of the Year.

Pablo Mastroeni was a different kind of defender. He was often more of a defensive midfielder, pressing the Rapids' attack forward. Mastroeni arrived in 2002, shortly after Balboa departed.

Mastroeni went on to become club captain and played in more games than anyone in team history. He was an All-Star in his first seven seasons. While not much of a goal scorer, Mastroeni did score a match-winner in the 2010 playoffs as Colorado marched to the first MLS Cup title in team history. He was a steady presence in the midfield for 11 seasons.

Three players have played 100 or more games in goal for Colorado. But only one has been there for a championship. Matt Pickens bounced around MLS and English soccer for years

Pablo Mastroeni, *right*, fights for the ball against Toronto FC's Maurice Edu.

before signing with Colorado in 2009. He became a starter for the team that won the 2010 MLS Cup.

Pickens made his first save just 19 seconds into that match. He allowed just one goal and made four other saves. Pickens left the club in 2014, but he remained the all-time leader in wins going into 2021.

PLAYMAKERS IN MIDFIELD

Chris Henderson joined Balboa on the original 1996 Rapids. He left after playing there for three years, but he returned for a second stint from 2002 to 2005. A creative playmaker and fan favorite, the midfielder racked up a club-record 53 assists in his time as a Rapid. Henderson was a two-time All-Star and team MVP of the inaugural Rapids.

Playing alongside Henderson on the team that made the 1997 MLS Cup was Paul Bravo. His 39 career goals were a team record until 2010. Bravo could score and was also great at setting up other scorers. He ranks in the top 10 in club history for both goals and assists.

Another American whose career predated MLS, Bravo retired as a player in 2001. He then joined the Colorado

Paul Bravo, *left*, challenges Jeff Agoos of DC United in 1999.

John Spencer, *left*, rarely shied away from a challenge.

coaching staff as an assistant in 2002. He later became the club's technical director.

ELECTRIC STRIKERS

It is hard to make a better entrance than John Spencer did. Spencer was a well-known player. He had played for years in the English Premier League with Chelsea and Everton. He signed with Colorado in 2001.

Spencer was near the end of his career, but he not washed up. He scored 14 goals with seven assists in that first year. He played in just 88 games in four seasons, but he scored 37 goals. That was fourth on the team's all-time list through 2020. Spencer was known as a fierce and fiery competitor. He was a favorite of fans and teammates, even serving as club captain.

Another striker with a knack for scoring goals, Conor Casey, was traded to the Rapids in 2007. Casey grew up in Colorado. But his pro career started in Germany. Casey struggled to get consistent playing time and opted to return to the North America. He signed with Toronto FC, who then traded him to Colorado.

Casey gradually developed his scoring touch. After scoring two goals in 15 matches in 2007, he scored 11 in 21 matches the next season. In 2010 he scored the 40th of his 50 career goals to become the club's all-time leading scorer. One of those goals came in the biggest match in team history, the 2010 MLS Cup. He was named MVP of the game.

Casey later became a Rapids assistant coach. In 2019 he filled in as head coach until the team hired Robin Fraser as its new head coach.

Colorado became home for forward Andre Shinyashiki, at least where soccer is concerned. Shinyashiki was born and raised in Brazil. But he moved to the United States to play high school soccer in Florida. He then went to the University of Denver to play college soccer.

Shinyashiki signed with the Rapids to play in their development academy. The Rapids then drafted him fifth overall in 2019. He scored a goal in his first appearance and added six more throughout the year. Shinyashiki was named MLS Rookie of the Year, just the second player to win in Rapids history.

The Rapids introduced Robin Fraser as their new head coach in August 2019.

CHAPTER 4

MILE HIGH
MEMORIES

Rapids fans were excited to see their brand-new team take the field in 1996. But some of that excitement faded when the club was shut out in its first match. The Rapids returned home after losing 3–0 in Kansas City.

Nonetheless, a crowd of 21,711 people gathered at Mile High Stadium. The match took on a party atmosphere. Fans kicked balls around in the parking lot. A parade of about 2,000 youth players got to take the field first.

Fans kept waiting patiently for the first goal in team history. Just after halftime, Marcelo Balboa got it done. Nine minutes later, Shaun Bartlett doubled the lead. The Dallas Burn cut the deficit in half, but Balboa got it back just minutes later. The crowd went home happy with a 3–1 win.

Marco Balboa makes a run for the Rapids in their first season.

The struggles of the inaugural season transformed into successes in the second season. The club had only a slightly better record from 1996. It even endured a late six-match losing streak. But the Rapids got into the playoffs, and that meant they had a chance.

Their first opponent, Kansas City, had beaten them in all four of their regular-season matchups. But Colorado turned the tables, winning 3–0 in the first game of the series. The Rapids then won the second match back at home 3–2 to advance.

They kept the ride going with a sweep of Dallas in the next round. They again won the second match at home. Chris Henderson scored the winner on a scissor kick goal in the 87th minute. Colorado went on to play DC United in its first MLS Cup.

The match was played in driving rain in Washington, DC. The Rapids let DC have some chances while trying to score on the counterattack. DC made the most of its chances, going up 2–0.

The Rapids finally scored in the 75th minute. A minute later, Wolde Harris had a golden chance to tie. He ran in alone on goal and fired a shot from 20 yards out. But he shot it high and

Chris Henderson plays the ball during the 1997 MLS Cup against DC United.

missed the goal completely. Colorado could not find another goal and lost 2–1.

CLOSING OUT MILE HIGH

Colorado played its last season in its original home of Mile High Stadium in 2001. A new version of Mile High Stadium opened the next season. John Spencer helped close out the old place in style on July 4, 2001.

July 4 is a special date on the Rapids schedule. The team traditionally plays at home and always draws a big crowd. More than 60,000 packed the stadium in 2001. Spencer was in his first season with the Rapids and had already scored a lot of big goals.

Just 48 seconds into the match, Spencer found the net for his first goal of the day. He went on to score two more. It was the first hat trick in club history.

The Rapids played five seasons in the new Mile High Stadium. But they began a new era in 2007 when they moved into their own home field. The stadium hosted big events that year. The Rapids played friendlies against top clubs from Mexico. It also hosted the MLS All-Star Game. But the biggest moment for Rapids fans was the first match at home.

John Spencer led the Rapids with 14 goals in 2001.

Dick's Sporting Goods Park opened on April 7, 2007. A sellout crowd of 18,086 was there to celebrate. Herculez Gomez scored the first goal and Roberto Brown added a second. Colorado beat DC United 2–1.

Shkelzen Gashi celebrates his goal in the second leg of the 2016 Western Conference semifinals against the LA Galaxy.

HEROES YOUNG AND OLD

The 2010 MLS Cup has to be the greatest match in Rapids history. But the greatest home match has a few contenders. Colorado has scored a few big playoff victories at home. But it is hard to top the second leg of the 2016 conference semifinals. The Rapids had been one of the top teams all season. They had the second-best record in all of MLS and hoped for a long playoff run. But then they lost the first leg of the conference semifinals 1–0 to the LA Galaxy. That meant they had to come home and win, or their season was over.

Shkelzen Gashi scored for the Rapids late in the first half. The aggregate score was tied 1–1. Jermaine Jones led the attack for Colorado. He worked hard to set up a winner, and the Rapids had several chances. But the match went to a penalty kick shootout.

HISTORIC UPSET

Colorado has generally not fared well in the US Open Cup, a tournament that US teams from all levels of play can enter. In its first 25 seasons, it only made the final one time, in 1999. That team lost to the minor-league Rochester Rhinos 2–0. Going into the 2021 event, that was the last time an MLS team did not win the cup.

After each team made its first kick, Giovani dos Santos stepped up for the Galaxy. He missed. Sébastien Le Toux scored for Colorado.

Ashley Cole was next for LA. Tim Howard stared him down. Howard had made big saves before in huge moments. Howard tracked where Cole was shooting. He dived to his right and made the save with his palm. Marco Pappa then scored for the Rapids. LA needed to score or it was over.

Jeff Larentowicz stepped up for the Galaxy. Howard sized him up. Again, he dived to his right. Again, Howard palmed away the attempt, clinching the victory for the Rapids.

Howard's teammates mobbed him as they celebrated in front of the home fans.

The magical run ended in disappointment. Colorado took a 1–0 lead in the first game of the conference finals against the Seattle Sounders. But it could not hold the lead and ended up losing both games by one-goal margins.

THE NEXT CHAPTER

Veterans Howard and Jones did not play in Colorado for long. The team set about building its next generation of stars. One 2019 game demonstrated that they were on the right track.

Sebastian Anderson was a homegrown Rapids player. He was not only from Colorado, he was signed and developed by the Rapids. He became the youngest signing in team history in April 2019. Weeks later, he became the youngest player in team history when he made his debut at 16 years, 262 days.

The record Anderson broke hadn't been around for long. His teammate Cole Bassett had set it less than a year earlier at age 17. In July Anderson became the youngest goal scorer in team history. That record had also belonged to Bassett.

Meanwhile, Andre Shinyashiki was the club's 22-year-old Rookie of the Year in 2019. One year later, Bassett and another

The Rapids are hoping to build their next championship team around young talent like midfielder Cole Bassett.

young player, forward Jonathan Lewis, tied for the team lead in goals as the Rapids returned to the playoffs. Despite a loss in the first round, the future was again looking bright in Colorado.

TIMELINE

1996	1997	1999	2001	2003
Colorado wins its inaugural home opener 3–1 over the Dallas Burn on April 21.	Colorado plays in its first MLS Cup on October 26 but loses 2–1 to DC United.	The Rapids make their first US Open Cup final but lose 2–0 to the Rochester Raging Rhinos on September 14.	John Spencer scores the first hat trick in team history on July 4 at Mile High Stadium.	On September 23, a group led by businessman Stan Kroenke announces plans to buy the Rapids from original owner Phil Anschutz.

2007	2007	2010	2016	2019
The team adopts a new badge and new colors of sky blue and burgundy.	The Rapids open Dick's Sporting Goods Park on April 7 with a 2–1 win over DC United.	Colorado wins its first championship in team history, beating FC Dallas 2–1 in the MLS Cup final in Toronto on November 21.	Colorado posts its best regular season in history, finishing with the second-best record in MLS.	Sixteen-year-old Sebastian Anderson becomes the youngest player in team history to score a goal when he finds the net against New York City FC on July 20.

TEAM FACTS

FIRST SEASON

1996

STADIUM

Mile High Stadium (1996–2001)
New Mile High Stadium (2002–06)
Dick's Sporting Goods Park (2007–)

MLS CUP TITLES

2010

KEY PLAYERS

Marcelo Balboa (1996–2001)
Paul Bravo (1997–2001)
Joe Cannon (2003–06)
Conor Casey (2007–12)
Omar Cummings (2007–12)
Chris Henderson (1996–98, 2002–05)
Tim Howard (2016–19)
Kei Kamara (2019–20)
Pablo Mastroeni (2002–13)
Matt Pickens (2009–13)
Andre Shinyashiki (2019–)
John Spencer (2001–04)

KEY COACHES

Robin Fraser (2019–)
Pablo Mastroeni (2014–17)
Glenn Myernick (1997–2000)

MLS ROOKIE OF THE YEAR

Dillon Powers (2013)
Andre Shinyashiki (2019)

MLS GOALKEEPER OF THE YEAR

Joe Cannon (2004)

MLS GOAL OF THE YEAR

Marcelo Balboa (2000)
Shkelzen Gashi (2016)

GLOSSARY

academy

A program run by a club to train young players and help them improve their skills.

aggregate

The combined score of both games in a two-game series.

bicycle kick

An acrobatic strike involving a player kicking an airborne ball over his or her head back toward the goal.

conference

A group of teams within a league.

extra time

Two 15-minute periods added to a game if the score is tied at the end of regulation.

friendlies

Matches that are not part of league play or a tournament; exhibition matches.

hat trick

Three goals by the same player in one game.

midfielder

A player who stays mostly in the middle third of the field and links the defenders with the forwards.

penalty shootout

A tiebreaking shootout of alternating kicks from the penalty spot that decides who wins the game.

rivalry

A fierce and ongoing competition between two players or teams.

rookie

A first-year player.

striker

A forward whose main job is to score goals.

veterans

Players who have played many years.

MORE
INFORMATION

BOOKS

Kortemeier, Todd. *Total Soccer*. Minneapolis, MN: Abdo Publishing, 2017.

Marthaler, Jon. *Ultimate Soccer Road Trip*. Minneapolis, MN: Abdo Publishing, 2019.

Trusdell, Brian. *Soccer Record Breakers*. Minneapolis, MN: Abdo Publishing, 2016.

ONLINE RESOURCES

Booklinks
NONFICTION NETWORK
FREE! ONLINE NONFICTION RESOURCES

To learn more about the Colorado Rapids, please visit **abdobooklinks.com** or scan this QR code. These links are routinely monitored and updated to provide the most current information available.

INDEX

ABOUT THE AUTHOR

Anthony K. Hewson has followed American soccer since before the MLS days. Originally from San Diego, he now lives in the Bay Area with his wife and dogs.